951
BRU

Bruycker, Daniel de.

470874

Tibet

$10.16

DATE DUE	BORROWER'S NAME	ROOM NO.

951
BRU

Bruycker, Daniel de.

470874

Tibet

977110 01016   30803A   001

Publisher's note:

Tintin, the intrepid reporter, first made his appearance January 10, 1929, in a serial newspaper strip with an adventure in the Soviet Union. From there, it was on to the Belgian Congo and then to America. Together with his dog, Snowy; an old seaman, Captain Haddock; an eccentric professor, Cuthbert Calculus; look-alike detectives, Thomson and Thompson; and others, Tintin roamed the world from one adventure to the next.

Tintin's dog, Snowy, a small white fox terrier, converses with Tintin, saves his life many times, and acts as his confidant, despite his weakness for whiskey and a tendency toward greediness. Captain Haddock, in some ways Snowy's counterpart, is a reformed lover of whiskey, with a tendency toward colorful language and a desire to be a gentleman-farmer. Cuthbert Calculus, a hard-of-hearing, sentimental, absent-minded professor, goes from small-time inventor to nuclear physicist. The detectives, Thomson and Thompson, stereotyped characters down to their old-fashioned bowler hats and outdated expressions, are always chasing Tintin. Their attempts at dressing in the costume of the place they are in make them stand out all the more.

The Adventures of Tintin appeared in newspapers and books all over the world. Georges Remi (1907–1983), better known as Hergé, based Tintin's adventures on his own interest in and knowledge of places around the world. The stories were often irreverent, frequently political and satirical, and always exciting and humorous.

Tintin's Travel Diaries is a new series, inspired by Hergé's characters and based on notebooks Tintin may have kept as he traveled. Each book in this series takes the reader to a different country, exploring its geography, and the customs, the culture, and the heritage of the people living there. Hergé's original cartooning is used, juxtaposed with photographs showing the country as it is today, to give a feeling of fun as well as education.

If Hergé's cartoons seem somewhat out of place in today's society, think of the time in which they were drawn. The cartoons reflect the thinking of the day, and set next to modern photographs, we learn something about ourselves and society, as well as about the countries Tintin explores. We can see how attitudes have changed over the course of half a century.

Hergé, himself, would change his stories and drawings periodically to reflect the changes in society and the comments his work would receive. For example, when it was originally written in 1930, *Tintin in the Congo*, on which *Tintin's Travel Diaries: Africa* is based, was slanted toward Belgium as the fatherland. When Hergé prepared a color version in 1946, he did away with this slant. Were Hergé alive today, he would probably change many other stereotypes that appear in his work.

From the Congo, Tintin went on to America. This was in 1931. Al Capone was notorious, and the idea of cowboys and Indians, prohibition, the wild west, as well as factories, all held a place of fascination. *Cigars of the Pharaoh* (1934) introduced Hergé's fans to the mysteries of Egypt and India. A trip to China came with *The Blue Lotus* in 1936, the first story Hergé thoroughly researched. After that, everything was researched, including revisions of previous stories. *The Land of Black Gold*, for example, an adventure in the Middle East, was written in 1939, and revised in 1949 and again in 1969. *The Black Island*, Tintin's adventure in Scotland, was published in black and white in 1938, in color in 1943, and updated in 1965. *Tintin in Tibet* began later. It came out in book form in 1960, thoroughly researched, down to the Yeti!

Although *The Broken Ear* introduced readers to the Amazon region in 1935, the story was pure fantasy, complete with imaginary countries. In 1974 the adventure continued with *Tintin and the Picaros*, Hergé's last story. When *The Seven Crystal Balls*, which was serialized from 1943 to 1944, was continued in 1946, Hergé began to give the reader factual information about pre-Columbian civilization with marginal notes titled "Who were the Incas?" *Tintin in the Land of the Soviets* was Tintin's first adventure, in 1929, and the only one not to be redone in color.

Tintin's Travel Diaries are fun to read, fun to look at, and provide educational, enjoyable trips around the world. Perhaps, like Tintin, you, too, will be inspired to seek out new adventures!

The publisher particularly wishes to thank Mrs. Christine Ockrent and television channel Antenne 2 for their kind permission to use the title *Travel Diaries*.

TIBET

TINTIN'S TRAVEL DIARIES

A collection conceived and produced by Martine Noblet.

Les films du sable *thank the following* **Connaissance du monde**
photographers for their participation in this work:

*Gilbert Leroy, René Vernadet, Oliver Berthelot,
Jean Ratel, and Louis Mahuzier*

*The authors thank Jérôme Edou,
Christiane Erard, and Pascale Dollfus for their collaboration.*

First edition for the United States and Canada published
by Barron's Educational Series, Inc., 1995.

All inquiries should be addressed to:
Barron's Educational Series, Inc.
250 Wireless Boulevard
Hauppauge, New York 11788

Library of Congress Catalog Card No. 95-17240

International Standard Book No. 0-8120-6504-2 (hardcover)
International Standard Book No. 0-8120-9237-6 (paperback)

Library of Congress Cataloging-in-Publication Data

Bruycker, Daniel de.
    Tibet / text by Daniel De Bruycker and Martine Noblet ;
translation by Maureen Walker.
        p.   cm. — (Tintin's travel diaries)
    Includes bibliographical references and index.
    Summary: Explores the history, geography, and culture of Tibet,
using Hergé's original cartooning along with modern photographs.
    ISBN 0-8120-6504-2. — ISBN 0-8120-9237-6 (pbk.)
    1. Tibet (China)—Description and travel—Juvenile literature.
2. Tibet (China)—Juvenile literature. [1. Tibet (China)
2. Questions and answers.] I. Noblet, Martine. II. Walker, Maureen.
III. Title. IV. Series.
DS786.B738   1995
951'.5—dc20   95-17240
                                                CIP
                                                AC

PRINTED IN HONG KONG
5678   9927   987654321

TIBET

Text by Daniel De Bruycker and Martine Noblet

Translation by Maureen Walker

BARRON'S

Mysterious Tibet! Just look at Tintin—he's telepathic. He can "hear" Chang calling to him for help. Then there's that lama with the extraordinary power of levitation, whose "spirit" has joined with Chang, the prisoner of the Yeti.

And there's another mystery: Chang, Tintin, and Captain Haddock are the only people in the world who have seen the Yeti!

Yes, with its great monasteries, its monks in their brightly colored clothing, and its inaccessible villages, this country—six times the size of Texas and surrounded by mountains—is very mysterious indeed, with much of its territory still unexplored. What will you young travelers discover about the eternal land of Tibet?

In 1951, the Chinese army invaded Tibet. Since 1966, China has been engaged in the systematic destruction of Tibetan culture, razing the forests, and humiliating and imprisoning the inhabitants. Will a "pure-hearted" man, a knight known in legends, come to save them? Will we find the will to help them at last?

GILBERT LEROY

As children, we spent many hours following Tintin, from adventure to adventure, around the world! When I was still a boy, I too drifted into long daydreams and discoveries in the footprints of my hero of that time. What is left of those pictures, those daydreams, that interest in foreign things? I thought I had left those books behind among my childhood memories, and then…! It happened one day in the fall. I had turned my footsteps toward the Himalayan uplands, to an area in Tibet about which I knew almost nothing. Drawn toward the tall hills overlooking the valley, I had climbed all the way up to the monastery. The place seemed deserted, except for the monk who greeted me, all smiles. Suddenly, I heard Tibetan horns roar, cymbals clash, and drums roll as lamas delivered their musical attack to drive away demons. As I was confronted by this unexpected sight, images from childhood came back to me and I smiled. Yes, of course—Tintin passed by here on his way to find Chang.

Several times since then, I have recognized myself—large as life—in pictures by Hergé. For instance, there was the day I was caught in a monsoon and took shelter under a carriage entrance in a dark district of Calcutta. I was waiting for the rain to stop when suddenly one section of the door opened. It was an opium parlor, the same as in *The Blue Lotus*. There I was, years after the days when I'd been so avid a reader of Hergé, rediscovering all the images that had fed my mind as a child. And there I was at last, actually in touch with the reality behind them.

OLIVER BERTHELOT

CONTENTS

Words in **boldface** in the text refer to the glossary on page 70.

WHY IS TIBET CALLED THE "ROOF OF THE WORLD"?

A huge, high plateau, six times the size of Texas, Tibet is surrounded by the highest mountains in the world. With an average elevation of 14,000 feet (4,400 m), it is the highest country on earth.

The continental drift brought into existence the natural fortress that is Tibet. Millions of years ago, India, with South America, Africa, Australia, and Antarctica, made up one continent called Gondwana. When this continent broke up, India drifted northward, crossing the Indian Ocean to eventually come to a stop against Asia, about 50 million years ago.

Although the continental drift progresses only a few fractions of an inch yearly, on the geologic scale this was a gigantic collision that completely changed the earth's topography for thousands of miles. The world's highest mountain ranges, the **Himalaya** and the **Karakoram**, resulted from this collision about 40 million years ago. The area that makes up present-day India sank beneath Asia, pushing up all of Tibet as far as the two mountain ranges (the Kunlun and the Altyn Tagh) that separate the country to the north from Chinese Turkestan. This movement is still occurring today, and although the rain and the winds are gradually planing down the peaks, the Himalaya and the Karakoram base is still pushing upward by a few fractions of an inch every year, with a dramatic rise of .8 inch (2 cm) a year for the Karakoram.

At the left is the western face of Everest
In the center is the snowy peak of Nuptse in Lhotse (Nepal)

WHO CONQUERED MOUNT EVEREST?

In 1953, the New Zealand mountain climber Edmund Percival Hillary and the Sherpa Tenzing Norgay reached the world's highest peak, Mount Everest—29,028 feet (8,848 m)—which rises in southern Tibet. The Tibetans call this peak Chomolungma, "Goddess Earth Mother."

Many mountain climbers have met their deaths—or achieved glory—by tackling Everest and the four other great peaks of the Himalaya. In 1950, Maurice Herzog conquered Annapurna in Nepal—26,500 feet (8,075 m)—but suffered severe frostbite on his hands and feet. In addition to the unbearable cold at such altitudes, climbers in Tibet are also confronted with the problem of getting people and equipment to the site with very rudimentary methods of transportation, as well as overcoming the famous mountain sickness that causes nausea so severe that it may result in death for anyone not used to breathing the rarefied air of the summits.

Most of the mountain climbers have had help from the **Sherpas**, mountain people who left Tibet in the fifteenth century to settle in Nepal, to the south of Mount Everest. The Sherpas cleared the high valleys and built small villages at altitudes between 11,375 and 13,650 feet (3,500 and 4,200 m). The mountain passes are sometimes so steep that the climbers can negotiate them only on foot, carrying their heavy loads on their backs.

It was only natural for the Sherpas to take part in the earliest expeditions. Efficient and pleasant, they have remained daring mountain dwellers who are capable porters and experienced guides for foreign climbers. Without them, the ascents would be impossible.

Edmund Percival Hillary of New Zealand and the Sherpa Tenzing Norgay, who conquered Everest

WHICH GREAT RIVERS HAVE THEIR SOURCES IN TIBET?

Tibet is a frozen desert where it rarely rains. But at the time of the summer thaw, the snow from the peaks feeds the springs of most of the principal rivers in Asia.

The Chang (formerly known as the Yangtze and sometimes erroneously called the Blue River) and the Huang He (Yellow River) flow eastward through all of China. The Chang River, which begins in the highlands of Tibet, is the longest river in Asia. The Mekong flows from Tibet through Vietnam; the Salween flows through Burma.

The Brahmaputra, considered the most important Tibetan river, empties into the Ganges delta in Bangladesh. The highest river in the world at 13,123 feet (4,000 m), it is also called the Tsangpo River. The Indus, passing through the western Himalayan range, flows down to Pakistan. Up on the Roof of the World, these huge rivers are wild, unnavigable mountain streams. They hollow out deep gorges in the rocks, and bridges, some of which are made of braided grasses, have been built over them.

The Brahmaputra detours more than 1,875 miles (3,000 km) around the Himalaya on the eastern side to reach the Indus plain, flowing through southern Tibet. Its valley and that of its tributary, the Kyichu River, are relatively fertile. Sheltered from the icy winds, they make up the most heavily populated area of the country.

On the high plateaus are the great lakes, several containing salt water. These lakes are part of the beauty of this country. The blue sky reflected in them makes them so impressive that they are honored as gods. Among them are Koko Nor, or Qinghai Hu, in the Chinese territory; Yam-drok-tso; and Manasarowar, at the foot of Kailash, the sacred mountain considered by Buddhists and Hindus to be the center of the world because it is thought to provide spiritual guidance and protection for the people of Tibet.

Top: A rope bridge in the Himalaya   Bottom: Lake Yam-drok-tso

WHICH ANIMALS ARE FOUND IN TIBET?

Whereas the black and white giant panda lives in the bamboo forests of southern China, its smaller cousin, with reddish fur and a long tail, can be found in the forests of eastern Tibet. This is the red, or lesser, panda, closely related to the raccoon.

There are 470 species of birds and 190 species of mammals on the Tibetan plateau. Some of them are threatened with extinction, among them the rare snow leopard, which is white with gray markings and smaller than the tropical leopard; the **wild yak**; and the black-necked crane, whose flavorful eggs have always been enjoyed by Tibetans. In the highlands live the Asiatic black bears, which may weigh as much as 246 pounds (120 kg); the Tibetan gazelle; the Himalayan marmot; and the ptarmigan, as well as vultures and some unusual insects, such as a caterpillar whose extract, the Tibetans believe, cures all ills. Other wild animals in Tibet include wild horses and tigers.

The salt marshes and lakes of the high plateaus are home to some unusual fish that have no scales. In summer, various species of geese and ducks can be found there. In the eastern valleys of the Himalaya, the climate is hot and humid. The virgin forest shelters the red panda, the small muntjac deer, and several species of monkeys.

Left: Black Asiatic bears
Right: A vulture

WHAT IS THE "ABOMINABLE SNOWMAN"?

In the Himalaya, there have always been tales of a mysterious creature, half-man, half-animal. Reported in China, Siberia, Tibet, and other mountainous areas, it has been nicknamed the "Abominable Snowman." The Sherpa people of Nepal call it the "Yeti."

By combining all the observations collected so far, we are able to get a fairly precise portrait of the Yeti. Half-man, half-ape, approximately 6 feet, 5 inches (2 m) tall, and covered with brownish fur, it is believed to have huge feet and bright eyes. It is said to leave footprints 16 inches (41 cm) long and 6 inches (15 cm) wide. This description would most likely make it some unknown species of primate or bear. Contrary to the legend, the Yeti is now said to live not in the snow, where it would be unable to find food, but in the very dense forests of Nepal, at an altitude of about 13,000 feet (4,000 m). There would seem to be nothing "abominable" about its character, for it is reportedly very shy and unaggressive.

Scientists have never been able to explain the mystery of the Yeti. This is not surprising, because even for a Tibetan or a Nepalese, the remote regions where it is said to live are difficult to reach and more or less uninhabited. The Yeti is said to exist in other mountainous regions, such as the Caucasus, Mongolia, and California, where it is called "Big Foot." It has also been reported in Oregon and the state of Washington, as well as British Columbia in Canada. Canadians call it "Sasquatch." Despite all the "sightings," however, there has never been any tangible sign that would convince skeptics of its existence.

Left: One of the peaks of the Himalaya
Right: Footprint of the "Abominable Snowman"

WHAT IS A YAK?

Standing more than 6 feet (1.8 m) high and weighing from 1,100 to 1,200 pounds (499 to 544 kg), covered with black or brownish-black hair, the wild yak is a ruminant with a massive body and a long coat. Without this animal, the Tibetans would be unable to navigate the icy heights of their country.

The yak is indispensable to the daily existence of the high-plateau Tibetan nomads. Wonderfully adapted to survival at a high altitude, robust and independent, it carries men and loads, swimming across rivers, if necessary, using its tail as a rudder. It is as agile as a mountain goat and can scramble up the steepest mountainside trails.

Winter and summer alike, the frigid cold, sharpened by the violent winds, is the worst enemy of the uplands Tibetans. In January, the average temperature is 24°F (–4°C). Temperatures in winter can go as low as –40°F (–40°C). The **domestic yak** is a wonderful ally in the cold climate. Besides its utility as a strong beast of burden, its long hair and hide are used to make ropes, clothing, tents, and boats. Its meat and the milk from the female yak (called *dri*) are staple foods. Yak butter is added to tea and is also used to protect hands and faces from frostbite. Finally, in this country with few trees, yak dung serves as fuel for the fires.

The yak is by far the best survival animal. To protect it from evil influences, its master hangs an amulet around its neck. When the yak dies, its meat is dried and its skin is tanned and used to make boots or bags. Its horns are placed on a hilltop as an offering to the gods, whereas its tail is fastened to one of the many prayer poles that mark the Tibetan landscape.

Top: Yak caravan
Bottom: A wild yak

ARE ALL TIBETANS NOMADS?

Many Tibetans are nomads, leading their flocks of yaks, sheep, and goats over the high plateaus. The others make their living by farming in the numerous valleys sheltered enough for barley and other crops to be grown in them. Still others live in the cities of Lhasa, Gyangze, Xigaze, and Yadong.

The **6 million Tibetans** call their country the "Land of Snow." Of the 2 million who live in the central province, most live in the south and in part of the eastern province of Kham. They are mainly cattle raisers, farmers, or traders. They travel their immense land on foot, on horseback, or astride their yaks, with heavily laden caravans, forever seeking fresh pastures.

Trade is based on the barter system. That is, the Tibetans exchange the surplus hair from their yaks or goats, the wool from their sheep, and their butter for manufactured goods, prayer books, silks, or jewelry.

In valleys in southern and eastern Tibet, where those who are not nomads live, there are some fertile areas in which apple and apricot trees flourish. The farmers grow barley, wheat, peas, and colza (rapeseed), from which they extract oil. The *dzo*, a cross between the domestic cow and the yak, serves as a beast of burden.

Top: Tibetan farmers
Bottom: Many Tibetans are still nomads

DO ALL TIBETANS LIVE IN TIBET?

At one time powerful, respected, and even feared by its neighbors, Tibet today has lost its independence and more than half its territory. Much of its population lives in exile.

King **Songzen Gampo**, who founded the city of Lhasa around C.E. 640, intimidated even the emperor of China with his fearless warriors. Since then, however, things have greatly changed, and the Roof of the World no longer dominates its neighbors. While the Tibetans, ruled by the **lamas** (spiritual leaders), devoted themselves to an exemplary spiritual life without material considerations, their neighbors took the offensive. First the Mongols, then the Manchus, took advantage of religious disputes to invade the country.

In the nineteenth century, the British (who were already established in India), the Russians, and the Chinese vied for domination of this poor but strategically important country. Its location in the very heart of Asia made it a considerable prize. Eventually, China triumphed, but in 1911, Tibetans were able to force out the Chinese troops. In the 1950s, China again gained control, and many Tibetans went into exile. China carved Tibet into three pieces, calling only the western part the "Tibet Autonomous Region."

Today, central Tibet has a population of 2 million Tibetans and more than 1 million Chinese. Four million more Tibetans live in exile in Chinese provinces and in Nepal, India, Bhutan, Sikkim, and other areas throughout the world. Tibetans are considered a minority in their own country.

Top and bottom left: The faces of Tibetans are usually dry, wrinkled, and prematurely old because of the sun, wind, and altitude
Bottom right: Tibetan children near Lake Yamdrok-tso

WHAT IS TREKKING?

Trekking is mainly making a long journey on foot. It means "walking on a trail." Tibetans have always traveled throughout their country in this way.

To go on a **trek** in Tibet is to walk all day, with a sack on one's back, climbing the majestic Himalaya, searching for fresh pastures, or seeing the magnificent scenery of the country. The true "trekkers" are the Sherpas who accompany groups of tourists on ascents in the Himalaya. Some of them are famous, as is, for example, Tenzing Norgay, the only man to have stood six times on Everest's summit.

Tibetans trek without realizing it. For them, it is simply the only way to travel. Traders trek in long caravans of several hundred yaks, receiving Indian or Chinese goods in exchange for yak wool, wild-animal pelts, butter, or barley flour. The pilgrims also travel the "Land of Snow," heading for Lhasa or Mount Kailash in trucks, on foot, or in a more unusual way, by prostration, whereby they lie flat on their faces at full length and get up again at the point where their hands touched the ground. They do this repeatedly for months, sometimes over a distance of 625 miles (1,000 km) or more.

These long journeys in the silence of the high mountains with their wild beauty have forged the character of this strong and intrepid people who are always in search of inner peace.

Top: Rope bridge reinforced with metal cables
Right: Tibetan foresters carrying loads on their backs

WHAT IS "TSAMPA"?

"Tsampa" is a flour made from ground, roasted barley. Mixed with salted tea with butter added to it, it is the basis of a Tibetan meal. In a land where fuel is scarce, it is especially desirable—it does not need to be cooked!

Salted tea with yak butter is the national drink of Tibet. With its high fat content, it helps the people tolerate the extreme cold. Dried yak meat, milk, and a cheese that keeps for years (children suck it as they might a hard candy) complete the diet of the nomadic herdsmen. In the valleys, the peasants add to this regular fare a few fruits and vegetables. On feast days, they prepare momos, which are large steamed dumplings filled with meat or vegetables. Any leftovers are fried the next day.

After 1970, the Chinese replaced the traditional cultivation of barley with that of winter wheat, which they prefer, but this cereal does not grow well at high altitudes and stops growing in cold weather. The drastic change led to famines that decimated the population. From barley, which is essential to them, Tibetans make a fermented drink called *chang*. They drink it during the long winter evenings when they gather as families or with neighbors to talk, laugh, and sing, or on special occasions, such as Losar, which begins the Tibetan New Year.

Top and bottom: Preparing a meal of *tsampa*, roasted barley flour

HOW DO TIBETANS TREAT ILLNESSES?

The Tibetans have developed their own way of treating illnesses, as well as medications derived from plants. In the past, the lamas studied this natural medicine at the Chakpori monastery in Lhasa.

Skilled herbalists and experts in reading their patients' pulses and analyzing urine, the lama physicians, called *amchis*, prescribe compresses and potions made from plants and minerals. They sometimes hold ceremonies during which they pray to exorcise demons, for it is their belief that some illnesses of the body are linked to those of the soul.

The lamas' knowledge of the human body is amazing. Before the eighth century, they practiced surgery, but it was later banned. Centuries before **Charles Darwin**, they developed a theory on the evolution of animal species. The herbalist lama physicians studied at the much renowned monastery of Chakpori, which is built on a hill facing the **Dalai Lama**'s palace, Potala. It was in this monastery that more than 500 different plants were collected, dried, ground to a powder, and then mixed according to ancestral recipes. Two modern drugs, based on old Tibetan formulas, are now being manufactured in Switzerland.

Since the destruction of the Chakpori monastery by the Chinese, the *amchis* can no longer get supplies of medications. Health issues continue to be one of the major problems in Tibet, where the incidence of infant mortality is around 50 percent. The new hospital at Lhasa is usually reserved for the Chinese or for tourists who are afflicted with the mountain sickness that results from lack of oxygen.

Top left: Tibetan dentist
Bottom left: Tibetan doctor spreading out his medicinal plants
Bottom right: Bottling medicinal plants and herbs

30

WHAT LANGUAGE DO TIBETANS SPEAK?

Although today Mandarin Chinese is the official language, Tibetans are still eager to speak and write their own language. It is a complex language, composed of many dialects, of which Lhasa is the most common.

The Tibetan language is a member of the Tibeto-Burman group of the Sino-Tibetan languages. There are about 10 million speakers, but the residents of every region speak their "own" Tibetan and each group has its own idiom. The ceremonial language spoken at the court of Lhasa where the Dalai Lama lived is beginning to disappear. Today, however, young Tibetan children try to learn how to write their alphabet in three graphic forms, including the one reserved for religious texts. These alphabets were invented around C.E. 650 by order of the king, Songzen Gampo, a convert to Buddhism, so that his subjects could read the words of Buddha.

Unfortunately, the harsh living conditions and the isolation of the nomadic populations living on the high plateaus prevent many children from attending school. Fewer than one-fourth of Tibetans study the sacred texts today. From 1959 to 1979, China prohibited the teaching of Tibetan in schools, and Chinese is still the official language in practice. Today, to get a job or start a business, a Tibetan is required to submit an application written in Chinese. Although official proclamations are written in both Mandarin and Tibetan, day-to-day internal documents are written only in Chinese.

Top: School for Tibetan exile monks in Ladakh
Bottom: Monks printing woodblock books

WHAT ARE TIBETAN MARRIAGE CUSTOMS?

Tibet is one of the last remaining countries where sometimes, by marrying the eldest man of the family, a woman also marries all his brothers!

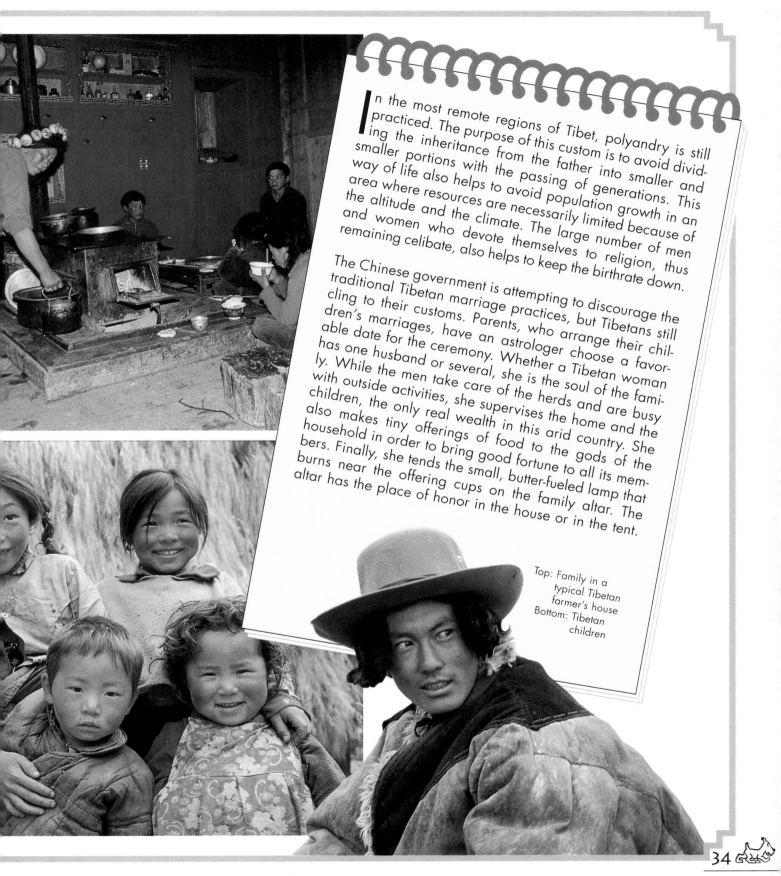

In the most remote regions of Tibet, polyandry is still practiced. The purpose of this custom is to avoid dividing the inheritance from the father into smaller and smaller portions with the passing of generations. This way of life also helps to avoid population growth in an area where resources are necessarily limited because of the altitude and the climate. The large number of men and women who devote themselves to religion, thus remaining celibate, also helps to keep the birthrate down.

The Chinese government is attempting to discourage the traditional Tibetan marriage practices, but Tibetans still cling to their customs. Parents, who arrange their children's marriages, have an astrologer choose a favorable date for the ceremony. Whether a Tibetan woman has one husband or several, she is the soul of the family. While the men take care of the herds and are busy with outside activities, she supervises the home and the children, the only real wealth in this arid country. She also makes tiny offerings of food to the gods of the household in order to bring good fortune to all its members. Finally, she tends the small, butter-fueled lamp that burns near the offering cups on the family altar. The altar has the place of honor in the house or in the tent.

Top: Family in a
typical Tibetan
farmer's house
Bottom: Tibetan
children

TO WHAT GODS DO TIBETANS PRAY?

Although the Tibetans adopted Buddhism, which came from India, about C.E. 650, they have not forgotten the spirits of nature and the awesome duties of their earlier religion, Bon.

Bon (pronounced "bone"), which may have derived from **Zoroastrianism**, itself supplanted **shamanism**, an older religion that is common to the peoples of Asia.

When Tibet became a powerful conquest empire, the rulers borrowed elements from Iranian state ritual that better suited the dynasty than local shamanism did. The Bon priests developed a sophisticated state cult, with animal sacrifices, elaborate burial rites, coronations, war ceremonies, and so on. After generations of successful conquest, the Tibetan kings began to look for arts of peace from more stable civilizations around them. They began to try to impose Buddhism on Tibet. They encountered strong resistance, resulting from opposition between Buddhist principles and the nationalistic religion of the Tibetans. For centuries, the Bon priests and the Buddhist monks vied for the favor of the Tibetans, torn between the noble wisdom of Buddhism and the power of the priests, who asserted that they could foretell the future, exorcise demons, and cure the sick. In the end, the two competing religions influenced each other.

The Bonpos, formerly lone magicians, became organized as a church with monasteries and religious texts. Meanwhile, Buddhist monks accepted the existence of evil spirits and the usefulness of magic to protect people from evil spells.

Top: Tibetan monks reading prayers
Bottom left: The faithful in the courtyard of the Jokhang sanctuary
Bottom right: Rock-painted icon outside Sera monastery

IS THERE A TIBETAN FORM OF BUDDHISM?

Buddha, the eminently wise, revered by more than 1 billion Asians, is surrounded in Tibet by several thousand divinities and spirits from ancient legends, Indian as well as Tibetan.

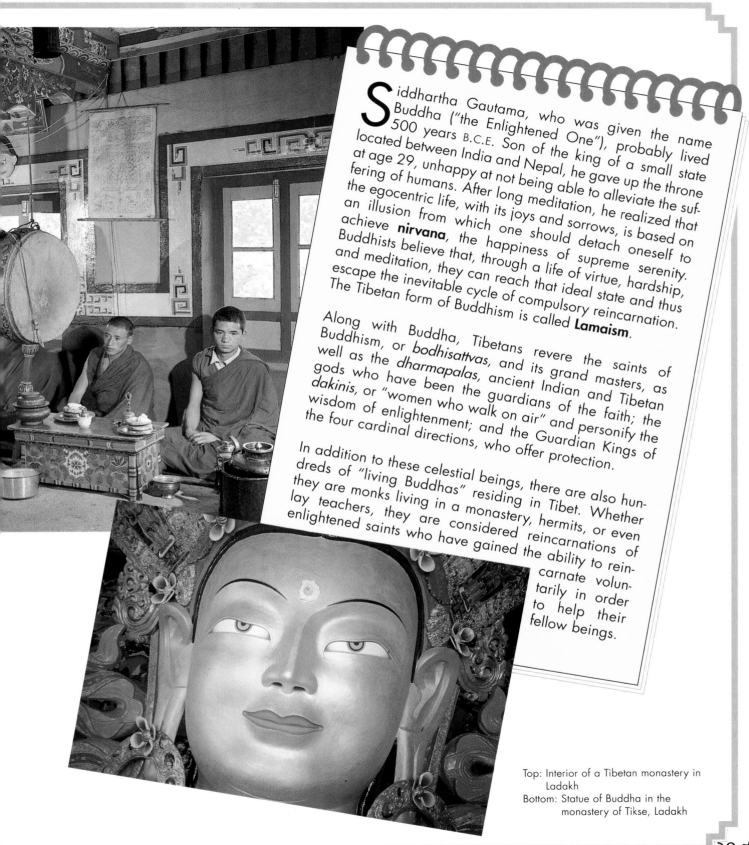

S iddhartha Gautama, who was given the name Buddha ("the Enlightened One"), probably lived 500 years B.C.E. Son of the king of a small state located between India and Nepal, he gave up the throne at age 29, unhappy at not being able to alleviate the suffering of humans. After long meditation, he realized that the egocentric life, with its joys and sorrows, is based on an illusion from which one should detach oneself to achieve **nirvana**, the happiness of supreme serenity. Buddhists believe that, through a life of virtue, hardship, and meditation, they can reach that ideal state and thus escape the inevitable cycle of compulsory reincarnation. The Tibetan form of Buddhism is called **Lamaism**.

Along with Buddha, Tibetans revere the saints of Buddhism, or *bodhisattvas*, and its grand masters, as well as the *dharmapalas*, ancient Indian and Tibetan gods who have been the guardians of the faith; the *dakinis*, or "women who walk on air" and personify the wisdom of enlightenment; and the Guardian Kings of the four cardinal directions, who offer protection.

In addition to these celestial beings, there are also hundreds of "living Buddhas" residing in Tibet. Whether they are monks living in a monastery, hermits, or even lay teachers, they are considered reincarnations of enlightened saints who have gained the ability to reincarnate voluntarily in order to help their fellow beings.

Top: Interior of a Tibetan monastery in
    Ladakh
Bottom: Statue of Buddha in the
    monastery of Tikse, Ladakh

WHAT ARE THE GREAT TIBETAN FESTIVALS?

From New Year's Day to the Great Evil Spirit Hunt that ends the year, Tibetans have many opportunities for coming together and rejoicing.

Many festivals take place at the time of the new or the full moon, for the lunar calendar is very important in Tibetan tradition. Most people honor the great deeds of Buddha's lifetime, especially his birth and the time of enlightenment that enabled him to overcome evil. During one of these celebrations, the Dalai Lama used to lead a procession around Lhasa, his whole court following; as he passed by, the Tibetans crowded around, even though looking at him was forbidden.

Other festivals deal with everyday life. During the September Ablutions Festival, also called the Golden Star Festival, the people of Lhasa purify themselves by bathing in the river. To celebrate the Feast of Chokor, meaning "blessing of the fields" and intended to ensure a rich harvest, Tibetans hold horse races and archery contests. The festival most revealing of the Tibetan character is the Incense Festival, held at the end of June, when, according to legend, hungry spirits pursue human beings. Because the spirits cannot attack anyone who is happy, the Tibetans join in a joyous, carnival-like celebration to escape the evil spirits. The festival often attracts mountain nomads to the cities and monasteries; it is also the occasion for holding a great market at which Tibetans can sell their cattle-raising products and make enough money to present an offering to the temple.

Top: Dance of the snow lions at a festival
Bottom: Pilgrims offering gifts to the Dalai Lama in the courtyard of the Kalachakra chapel

WHAT ROLE DOES MUSIC PLAY IN TIBET?

In Tibet, dance and music are important to religious observances. At ritual ceremonies, horns and drums are used to chase away demons and to attract the attention of the gods.

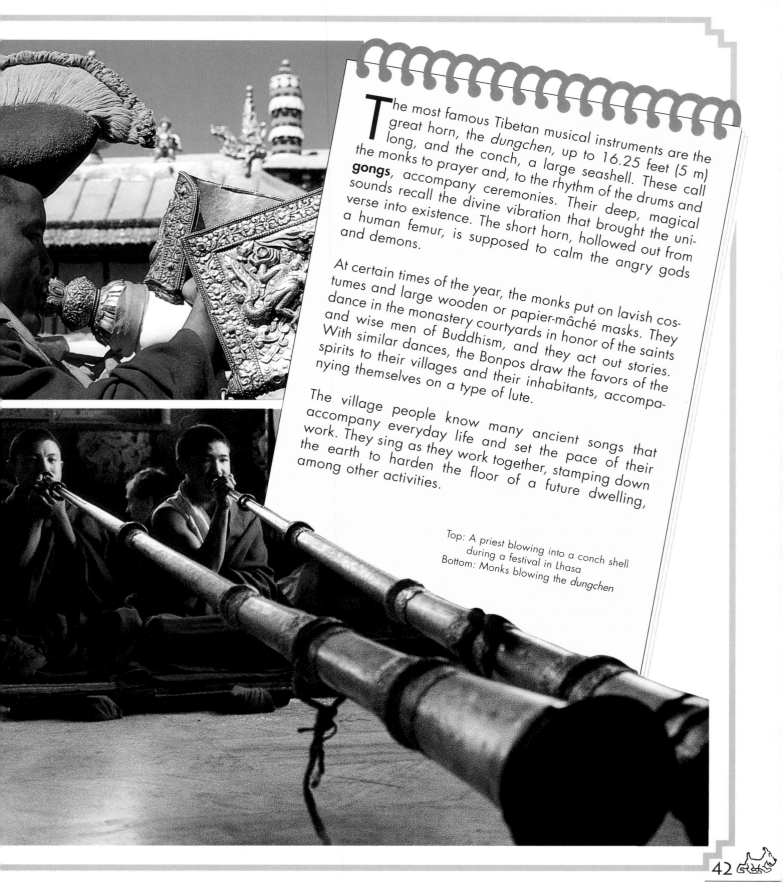

The most famous Tibetan musical instruments are the great horn, the *dungchen*, up to 16.25 feet (5 m) long, and the conch, a large seashell. These call the monks to prayer and, to the rhythm of the drums and **gongs**, accompany ceremonies. Their deep, magical sounds recall the divine vibration that brought the universe into existence. The short horn, hollowed out from a human femur, is supposed to calm the angry gods and demons.

At certain times of the year, the monks put on lavish costumes and large wooden or papier-mâché masks. They dance in the monastery courtyards in honor of the saints and wise men of Buddhism, and they act out stories. With similar dances, the Bonpos draw the favors of the spirits to their villages and their inhabitants, accompanying themselves on a type of lute.

The village people know many ancient songs that accompany everyday life and set the pace of their work. They sing as they work together, stamping down the earth to harden the floor of a future dwelling, among other activities.

Top: A priest blowing into a conch shell during a festival in Lhasa
Bottom: Monks blowing the *dungchen*

WHAT DO TIBETAN CHILDREN FEAR?

From the time they are very young, Tibetan children tell each other frightening tales about "mimayin," invisible ghosts that haunt the valleys and the hills, always looking for an outlet for their anger.

Tibetan children are taught that, aside from the visible world, there exists another universe, one filled with creatures that are just as real—the *mimayin*. Although invisible, the *mimayin* are never very far away, having escaped from one of the hells where people who misbehave are scalded, chopped into little pieces, or frozen on the mountaintops. It is said that the *mimayin* are the spirits of people who died without ever having carried out a vow, gotten revenge for an injustice, or repented of an evil deed. They inhabit a lake or a mountain.

The benevolent deities protect peasants and their harvests, but when they are angry, they appear in the form of monsters. They can cast cruel spells on the enemies of Buddhism and use their sabers to pierce through ignorance. It is to appease them that people avoid fishing in the rivers and plant prayer flags beside the lakes, on the hills, or in the mountain passes. Those are all solitary places to which even adults do not go without fear, and they serve as an excellent incentive for young Tibetans to behave all the time and not venture too far from the village by themselves!

Top: Each monastery has its own guardian deities
Bottom left: The guardian king of the West
Bottom right: Tibetan child

ARE THERE CEMETERIES IN TIBET?

Instead of being buried, Tibetans prefer the body to be closer to the sky. They are therefore cremated or fed to birds of prey while the family prays to help the deceased on the journey to the beyond.

When someone dies, a monk is instructed to accompany that person's spirit toward the other world on the journey through the dangerous regions before he or she can be reborn. The texts of the Bardo, or Book of the Dead, are recited to warn the deceased of the dangers that are likely to be met and to advise the deceased on the way to behave in order to obtain a good reincarnation.

The mortal remains are blessed; wrapped, in a sitting position, in a shroud; placed on the mountains in a consecrated place; and then cut into pieces to be devoured by vultures. The poor and children who have died are simply put in the rivers. In Tibet, it is believed that the human body is valuable only because of the life that resides in it. Once that life is extinguished, the body can be useful to other living beings, such as birds, mammals, or fish.

Because wood is valuable and scarce, cremation is reserved for the bodies of grand masters and lamas so that their ashes, placed in an urn under a **chorten**, will spread good to all. High dignitaries are embalmed. Their bodies, sometimes covered with gold, become relics that will remind pilgrims of the importance of the dignitaries' teachings.

Top: Monks reciting a Tantric ritual
Bottom: Steeple reconstructed below Ganden monastery

WHAT IS A MANDALA?

A mandala is much more than just a picture; it is a depiction of the sacred circle of the enlightened life. For the faithful, who meditate while contemplating its complex geometric design, the mandala is a map capable of guiding them in the direction of wisdom.

In the center of the image, the mandala, which means "essence of reality," depicts deities. Around the outside are circular or square enclosures that contain pictures of people or symbols, up to the triple outer circle, which is painted with multicolored flames, lotus petals, and so forth.

The faithful, who meditate while concentrating on the mandala according to precise rules, try to visualize themselves inside the pictured space as close as possible to its center, from which they then receive the sacred power.

Mandalas may be formed on the ground with hand-colored sand or painted on cloth from which *thangkas* are made. *Thangkas* are rectangular-shaped religious paintings put on fabric bordered by brocade, with colors that are produced by a secret process. Once the mandalas have been blessed, they have immense power. Even the water used to wash a mirror in which *thangkas* are reflected is believed to have great power.

Tibetans have other sacred objects, such as rosaries made up of 108 beads, on which they count mantra, secret prayers or incantations. They also have reliquaries, a type of jewelry that may contain a relic or a picture of the Dalai Lama.

In addition, there are sacred objects of impressive size, such as the walls of Mani, prayer-engraved dry stone walls, some of them several miles long, around which, as with all the sacred monuments, the people walk in a clockwise direction.

Top: A mandala made of colored sand that is scattered over the river after ten days
Bottom: A guardian king deity at the entrance to a temple

WHAT IS THE KATA?

During pilgrimages, an important part of the rituals is the offering at the temple of a white silk scarf called a "kata."

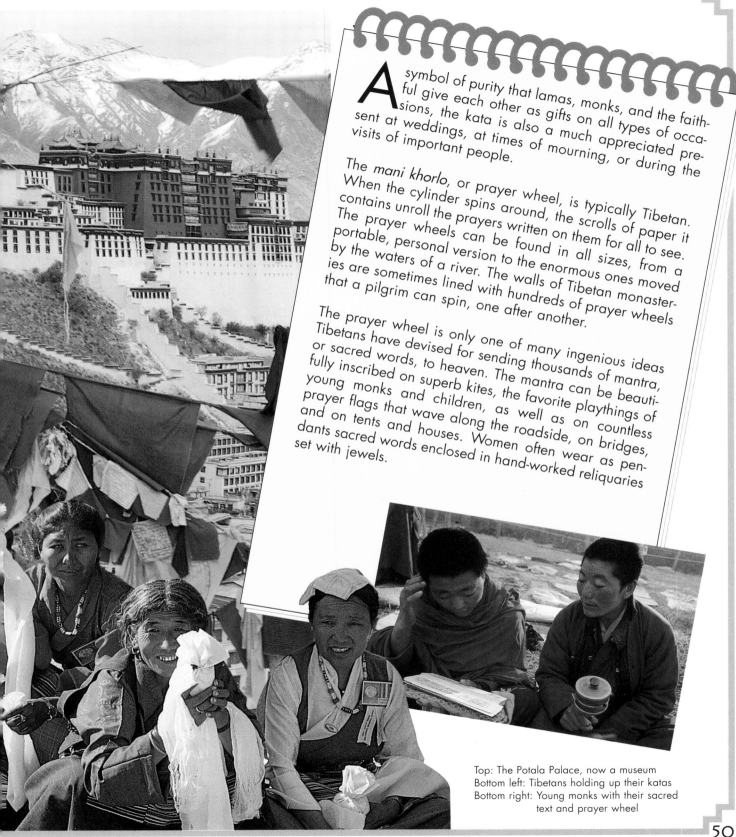

A symbol of purity that lamas, monks, and the faithful give each other as gifts on all types of occasions, the kata is also a much appreciated present at weddings, at times of mourning, or during the visits of important people.

The *mani khorlo*, or prayer wheel, is typically Tibetan. When the cylinder spins around, the scrolls of paper it contains unroll the prayers written on them for all to see. The prayer wheels can be found in all sizes, from a portable, personal version to the enormous ones moved by the waters of a river. The walls of Tibetan monasteries are sometimes lined with hundreds of prayer wheels that a pilgrim can spin, one after another.

The prayer wheel is only one of many ingenious ideas Tibetans have devised for sending thousands of mantra, or sacred words, to heaven. The mantra can be beautifully inscribed on superb kites, the favorite playthings of young monks and children, as well as on countless prayer flags that wave along the roadside, on bridges, and on tents and houses. Women often wear as pendants sacred words enclosed in hand-worked reliquaries set with jewels.

Top: The Potala Palace, now a museum
Bottom left: Tibetans holding up their katas
Bottom right: Young monks with their sacred text and prayer wheel

WHAT IS A TIBETAN BUDDHIST MONASTERY?

Patterned on the huge Buddhist monastic universities of ancient India, such as Nalanda, Tibetan monasteries are institutions for celibate monks and nuns.

Physically, Tibetan monasteries often resemble fortresses clinging to mountain slopes. Before the Chinese invaded Tibet, the place of the monasteries in political, economic, and cultural life was similar to that of cities in our society. Though many of them were only isolated, ramshackle buildings, the principal monasteries, in which thousands of religious people lived, were actual cities. Often rich from the alms of the faithful, they had officials to maintain order, thus encouraging caravans to stop there as a refuge from thieves. These monasteries were often endowed by the government with gifts of land, increasing their wealth even more. The monasteries had an administrative system for collecting taxes and rents and selling the sacred objects they made.

The monks, and especially their lama-teachers, are one of the two elites of the population, along with the landed aristocracy. Before the Chinese took over, 20 percent of Tibetan men were monks. Some families sent their children to the monasteries for a better life. Others went there for education. Today the few monks that remain must engage in agriculture and crafts. The monasteries are centers for education and art, as well as worship. A monastery will accept a novice at any age, if a friend or relative takes responsibility for finding a master and housing. He will share his time among work, study, and religious ceremonies from dawn until late into the night.

In 1950, there were over 6,000 monasteries in Tibet. Today, only 13 remain; the Chinese destroyed the others.

Top: Debating contest among the monks in the ruins of the Ganden monastery   Bottom: Monks praying at a monastery near Lhasa

WHAT IS THE POTALA?

The Potala is the fortress-palace that was once the home of the Dalai Lama. Built by the fifth Dalai Lama in the seventeenth century on the red hill of Lhasa, this imposing edifice, with its height of 380 feet (117 m), towers over the capital.

Around the seventh century C.E., the kings of Tibet dominated all of central Asia, but they quickly lost their prestige, and their power was undermined by struggles among the clans and between the followers of the ancient Bon cult and the new Buddhist religion.

The Buddhists, whose monasteries controlled vast domains, began to exercise political power in the thirteenth century. They remained in power until the Chinese invasion, despite rivalry among the various orders. In this "buddhacratical" system, in which supreme power belongs to the Buddhas, the monks and their abbots shared with aristocratic laymen most of the key positions: civil servants, judges, provincial and district governors, and so on. Since the seventeenth century, all have owed obedience to the Dalai Lama, the supreme head of both government and Buddhism, who lived in the huge Potala at Lhasa in the midst of his priestly court and members of his government.

The palace, a 13-story structure, had more than 1,000 rooms, 10,000 altars, 200,000 statues, libraries of inestimable worth, and treasure chambers. Building it was a huge undertaking—spanning nearly sixty years, from 1637 to 1696. The Tibetans, who did not maintain a road system for wheeled vehicles, had to bring in the building materials on the backs of yaks and donkeys and men, a difficult task because the walls of the Potala, ranging from 16.5 to 13 feet (2 to 4 m) thick, are strengthened with copper castings for protection against the frequent earthquakes. The Potala is now a state museum with thirty-five caretakers.

The Potala Palace

24

WHY WERE FOREIGNERS BARRED FROM LHASA?

A city that was once inaccessible to foreigners, Lhasa, the capital of Tibet, remained a mystery for many years. It was called the "Forbidden City." Until 1860, the rest of the world was unaware of its precise location, because no geographers had ever reached it.

In the eighteenth century, all that was known in the West about Lhasa were a few descriptions by Jesuit and Capuchin missionaries who had traveled in the country. The lamas, eager to protect Tibet from all foreign influences they considered harmful to the spiritual growth of their people, were successful in keeping Tibet out of the turmoil of modern life. But the price of this isolation was a total absence of technological progress. In 1945, the number of automobiles and buildings equipped with electricity was very small. The telephone and airplane were entirely unknown in this huge country, where the lifestyle was still medieval.

It was therefore not very hard for neighbors as powerful as the Chinese or the British, who were settled in India, to influence the destiny of a relatively primitive country. Around 1811, an eccentric Englishman, Thomas Manning, had managed to enter Lhasa by chance, disguised as a Chinese physician. Actually, he had intended to sneak into Beijing. Then, at the end of 1903 a British military expedition of barely 1,200 men, led by Francis Younghusband, forced its way into the city, massacring some 700 Tibetans, and set up a consulate there. In 1923, Alexandra David-Neel, a French Orientalist, became the first European woman to enter Lhasa.

Today, Lhasa has a population in excess of 150,000 people, two-thirds of them Chinese. It has stone-and-brick houses and shops and many monasteries and temples.

Top: The Potala at the beginning of the twentieth century
Bottom: French Oriental scholar and writer Alexandra David-Neel and a lama in Tibet around 1920

HOW IS THE DALAI LAMA CHOSEN?

Tibetans recognize one Grand Lama: the Dalai (High) Lama, considered the ruler of Tibet and its spiritual leader. The Panchen Lama is another high spiritual authority. Both are thought to have the power to reincarnate consciously. Tibetans believe that when the Dalai Lama or the Panchen Lama dies, he changes bodies and is reincarnated with all his powers in the person of a child somewhere in Tibet.

The first Dalai Lama, Gendun Drup, was born in 1391. The thirteenth Dalai Lama died in 1933. The government consulted the state oracles and the most erudite of the lamas to determine where he could have been reincarnated. They interpreted a number of signs. The body of the deceased Dalai Lama had been displayed, seated upon his throne, facing south. A few days later, his face was turned eastward. For the oracles, it was obvious they must look for a new Dalai Lama in that direction.

In 1937, in a small village in the Amdo region of northeastern Tibet, two mendicant monks came to the house of a peasant family to observe a two-year-old boy. They questioned him skillfully, and the boy answered with great composure. He knew the name of the head of a great Lhasa monastery and recognized certain hidden items that had belonged to the thirteenth Dalai Lama. Two years later, the child was accepted as the fourteenth reincarnation of the Dalai Lama. He was taken to Lhasa with his family and showered with honors. The child was enthroned in 1940, at the age of five. In order for him to "relearn" the knowledge accumulated in his previous lives, he was entrusted to the most learned masters in Tibet.

The Dalai Lama, who has lived in exile in India since 1959, is head of the Gelukpa order of Tibetan Buddhism. He has always worked to end Chinese rule through nonviolent means. The **Panchen Lama**, after fifteen years in Chinese prisons, favored unity with China. He died in the Tashilhunpo monastery in 1989.

Top: Young monk seated in the small temple in Lhasa
Bottom: Tibetan student monks reading their alphabet

WHO RULES TIBET TODAY?

Upon the invasion of the country in 1950, the old religious regime was swept away by the Chinese occupying power. Today, Tibet is an "autonomous" region governed by the Chinese. Since 1965, its specific name has been the "Tibet Autonomous Region of the People's Republic of China." It is also called Xizang.

The Dalai Lama, then only 15, tried to resist the Chinese invasion, but his army of 8,000 inexperienced men was ineffective against the power of the invaders.

Even though not all of the Tibetan people entirely opposed the modernization of the country, it soon became clear that the stated will of the Chinese to "free Tibet of the tyranny of the religious" in fact disguised the desire of the Chinese to increase their own territory and power.

The intolerance of the Chinese Communist regime, persecuting the lamas and destroying thousands of monasteries, profoundly shocked this deeply devout people. Although China has built schools, hospitals, and factories and has opened up highways, this infrastructure is useful mainly to the Chinese colonists, who are settling on lands confiscated from the monasteries and aristocratic families.

The prohibition against teaching in the Tibetan language and engaging in barter, which has always been the basis of trade in Tibet, was typical of a Chinese attitude that quickly roused all of Tibet against the invader. In 1959, when China violently repressed a Tibetan protest movement by shelling Lhasa, the Dalai Lama was forced to flee his oppressed country. In 1980, holy sites were reopened and cultural restrictions were eased somewhat until martial law was again imposed between 1989 and 1992. Protests began again in 1993 and continue sporadically.

Top left: Inscriptions on the fronts of a shop in Lhasa (in Chinese and Tibetan)
Bottom left: The Chinese are everywhere in Lhasa
Bottom right: Chinese soldiers driving a truck marked "Drepung Monastery"

27

WHAT NATURAL RESOURCES ARE FOUND IN TIBET?

Obedient to the lamas and more concerned about spiritual progress than modernization, Tibetans have never taken advantage of their huge forests and the riches to be found in their land.

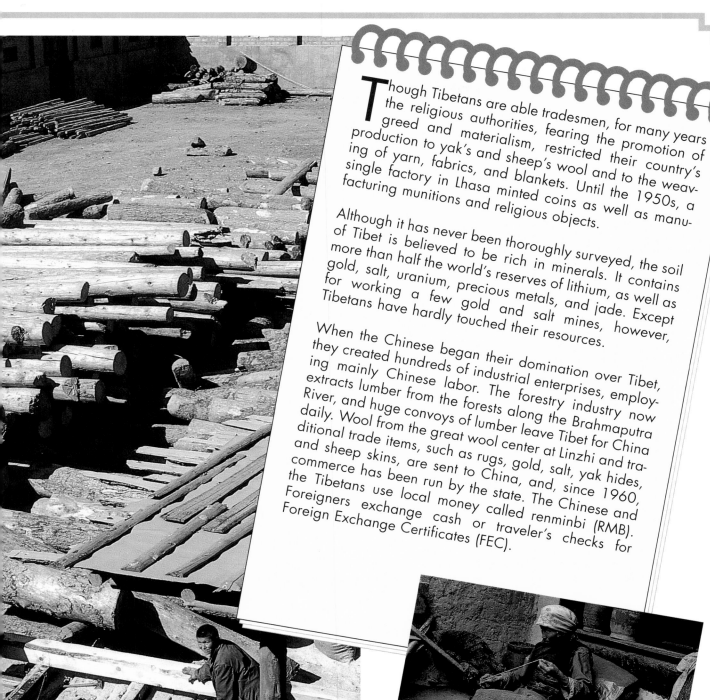

Though Tibetans are able tradesmen, for many years the religious authorities, fearing the promotion of greed and materialism, restricted their country's production to yak's and sheep's wool and to the weaving of yarn, fabrics, and blankets. Until the 1950s, a single factory in Lhasa minted coins as well as manufacturing munitions and religious objects.

Although it has never been thoroughly surveyed, the soil of Tibet is believed to be rich in minerals. It contains more than half the world's reserves of lithium, as well as gold, salt, uranium, precious metals, and jade. Except for working a few gold and salt mines, however, Tibetans have hardly touched their resources.

When the Chinese began their domination over Tibet, they created hundreds of industrial enterprises, employing mainly Chinese labor. The forestry industry now extracts lumber from the forests along the Brahmaputra River, and huge convoys of lumber leave Tibet for China daily. Wool from the great wool center at Linzhi and traditional trade items, such as rugs, gold, salt, yak hides, and sheep skins, are sent to China, and, since 1960, commerce has been run by the state. The Chinese and the Tibetans use local money called renminbi (RMB). Foreigners exchange cash or traveler's checks for Foreign Exchange Certificates (FEC).

Left: Taking lumber from the forests of the Kham province
Right: Working with wool

28

WHO ARE THE KHAM-PA?

In eastern Tibet, the Kham-pa, or people of Kham, would rob the merchant caravans passing through their territory. But these "highwaymen," who are devoutly religious and very attached to their particular code of honor, are anything but common thieves.

Common thieves are rare in Tibet. Stealing a yak from a nomad or grain from a peasant can mean bearing the responsibility for the deaths of those people and their families.

Easily recognizable by the topknots of red yarn woven into their hair, the Kham-pa have always terrorized their neighbors. But ever since the Chinese invaded their province, the Kham, and tried to disarm these tribes of proud horsemen, the Kham-pa have never stopped rebelling, despite the fact that the enemy is much more powerful than they are. The courageous resistance of this warlike people has earned the respect of many Tibetans.

In 1956, the Chinese army, still fighting the Kham-pa, shelled one of their great monasteries in which thousands of monks and peasants had taken refuge. More than 15,000 families then fled toward Lhasa and toward the south, where people from all over Tibet joined them to fight. They made up the group "from the four rivers and the six mountains" and resisted Chinese occupation until Nepal destroyed the Tibetan bases established in Mustang, one of its districts.

Top: A refugee Kham-pa
Bottom left: Kham-pa traders in Lhasa
Bottom right: Nomad shepherd

29

WHY ARE TIBETANS IN REVOLT AGAINST CHINA?

Deprived of their freedom and forced to give up their religion and their way of life by the Chinese, who are exploiting the natural resources of their country, the Tibetans, not surprisingly, dream of regaining their independence.

More than 1 million Tibetans have lost their lives because of the Chinese occupation. To the genocide and almost total destruction of the monasteries have been added the first great famines in Tibet's history. Not content with confiscating the bulk of the harvests to feed its army of occupation and its colonists, China decided to reform agriculture. Flocks and fields were turned into collectives, and farmers were forced to plant not barley but wheat, which is preferred by the Chinese but unsuited to the climate of Tibet.

The large wool output is now sent to mills where only Chinese workers are employed. China has also taken over the mines, banks, newspapers, and food stores. The Chinese hold most of the jobs as local government administrators and teachers, and they discriminate against the Tibetans.

Today, some restrictions have been lifted. Farming, animal raising, and crafts are being practiced more freely, and some monasteries have been allowed to reopen. Fearing that this may be only a stage setting designed to persuade Western countries that the Chinese occupation is good for Tibet, however, Tibetans, led by the Dalai Lama in exile, continue to address appeals to the United Nations for restoration of their country's independence.

Left: A monk throws a stone during the riots of October 1, 1987   Right: The ruined monastery of Ganden in the Lhasa Valley

30

WHERE IS THE DALAI LAMA?

Since his exile in 1959, the fourteenth Dalai Lama has lived as a refugee at Dharamsala in India, where he continues to call for the independence of his country. Opposing all violence, he has always called for world peace, and in 1989 he was awarded the Nobel Peace Prize.

With the help of a number of humanitarian organizations, the Dalai Lama and his government in exile are building reception centers for refugees, as well as schools where the traditional culture is taught.

At Dharamsala, the ancient schools of medicine and pharmacy have been re-created. The most famous of the Tibetan monasteries—Drepung, Ganden, Sera, and others—have been reestablished in southern India, and others in Nepal. The Dalai Lama is trying to preserve the culture of his country while waiting for the day when it will be able to flourish once again on the Roof of the World. While negotiating—unsuccessfully, so far—with the Chinese government, the Dalai Lama has been attempting to make the rest of the world aware of the sad situation of his people, but he does not encourage armed rebellion. He prefers to rely on the power of prayer and, in negotiations with China, on patience and moderation. He also depends on the respect millions of people throughout the world—not only Tibetans—have for him because of his great wisdom and his pacifism.

Left: Tenzing Gyatso, the fourteenth Dalai Lama, in exile in India
Right: A young Tibetan girl holding a photo of the Dalai Lama

B

BON: the religion that preceded Buddhism and competed with it. Today, Bon contains doctrines that are almost identical to those of Tibetan Buddhism and deals with magic and the exorcism of evil spirits as well.

C

CHORTEN: also known as *stupa*, a shrine or commemorative monument in the shape of a full dome, raised over relics of the Buddha or prominent religious people. The *chorten* is a carryover from Indian Buddhism.

D

DALAI LAMA: (title) conferred since 1578 on the heads of the Gelukpa order of Tibetan Buddhism. From 1642 until 1950, the Dalai Lama was the political and spiritual ruler of Tibet. Tenzing Gyatso, born in 1935, was enthroned in 1940 as the fourteenth Dalai Lama. When the revolutionary Chinese troops invaded Tibet in 1950, he was forced to surrender the country when the United Nations would not respond to his appeal. In 1959, after a revolt in Tibet, he took refuge in India, where he remains today, spreading the story of the plight of his people to the world and preaching nonviolence.

DARWIN, CHARLES ROBERT (1809–1882): British naturalist who played a major role in the biological sciences with theories on evolution. He believed all plants and animals came from a few common ancestors. Darwin worked out a system of philosophy designed to explain the development of the species by emphasizing natural selection and the survival of the fittest.

G

GONG: percussion instrument consisting of a suspended metal plate that is struck with a padded drumstick. The gong is used in Tibetan religious ceremonies.

H

HIMALAYA: "House of Snow." Huge mountain range extending over an area 1,500 miles (2,410 km) long across southern Asia. It is a natural barrier separating northern India from the Plateau of Tibet, in China. Some parts of the range are as much as 200 miles (320 km) wide.

K

KARAKORAM (MUSTAGH) RANGE: "Black Stone." Very high mountainous system that includes the Karakoram and three other ranges in the western Himalaya. K2 (28,250 feet [8,611 m] high), located in the Karakoram Range, is the world's second highest mountain.

L

LAMA: in Tibetan, "spiritual teacher." The term, from the Sanskrit for "guru," refers to a highly learned Tibetan Buddhist monk, nun, or lay priest. In order to achieve enlightenment, one must be initiated by a lama, as a true lama teaches spiritual awakening to his or her disciples. Lamas can be female, although the majority are male. Western writers have created confusion by referring to all Tibetan monks and nuns as "lamas," leading to the misnomers "Lamaism" and "lamaseries." All Buddhists have great reverence for learned spiritual teachers, and all Buddhist monks and nuns live in monastic cloisters. The Tibetan monasteries are the largest in the world. Tibet is also the only Buddhist country where the monasteries took the lead role in administering the government and a monk served as ruler. Since a monk cannot leave children to succeed him, the Tibetans developed the unique system of succession by reincarnation.

LAMAISM: a synthesis of Monastic Buddhism; Mahayana, or Social Buddhism; and Vajrayana, or Esoteric Buddhism. It contains four major orders, the most important of which is the Gelukpa, or Yellow Hat order, headed by the Dalai Lama.

N

NIRVANA: "loss of pain." In Buddhism, nirvana may be considered a state of supreme serenity, leading to the end of the cycle of death and rebirth. In order to achieve nirvana, Buddhists renounce worldly desires and possessions.

P

PANCHEN LAMA: the reincarnation of the fifth Dalai Lama's teacher. He is regarded by the Tibetan people as a high spiritual authority and, along with the Dalai Lama, believed to be a reincarnation of a Buddha. In 1959, when the Dalai Lama fled to India, the tenth Panchen Lama became vice-chairman of a committee to establish Tibet as an autonomous region. When he refused to denounce the Dalai Lama and serve as a spiritual figurehead under the Chinese, he was jailed from 1963 to 1978. After his release, he favored unity with China. He died in 1989, in the Tashilhunpo monastery, during the wave of protests at the Chinese reimposition of martial law.

S

SHAMANISM: a religion in which there is a belief in an unseen world of gods, demons, and ancestral spirits who respond only to *shamans*, priests who go into trances to cure illness, excoriate demons, or communicate with spirits.

SHERPAS: members of a Tibetan mountain-dwelling tribe. Accustomed to the harsh Himalayan climate and to high altitudes, Sherpas are often guides in Himalayan expeditions. They are traditionally farmers, growing potatoes, barley, corn, and wheat, and raising yaks. Their language is a Tibetan dialect, and they practice Tibetan Buddhism.

6 MILLION TIBETANS: There are an estimated 6 million Tibetans scattered over a number of countries. Under Chinese domination since 1950, about one half of former Tibet is known today as Xizang, the "Tibet Autonomous Region of the People's Republic of China," its official name since 1965. It forms the southwestern part of China. Two million Tibetans live there. Other Tibetans live in Chinese provinces; in Nepal, India, Sikkim, and Bhutan; and in small communities in Europe, Canada, and the United States.

SONGZEN GAMPO: king (circa 605–649) who provided his kingdom with centralized organization. He extended his power toward Nepal and India. During his reign, the Tibetan written language was created and the first Buddhist temples were built in Tibet. His two wives, one Chinese and the other Nepalese, contributed to the introduction of Buddhism, particularly to Lhasa, which he established as the capital.

T

THANGKAS: mobile scroll paintings or cloth icons showing a religious picture.

TREK: originally an Afrikaans term meaning "a slow or difficult journey," "a day's travel," or "an expedition."

Y

YAK, DOMESTIC: also called "grunting ox." Smaller than the wild yak, this bovine is often white or piebald and is found throughout the mountainous regions of central Asia.

YAK, WILD: a bovine remarkably well adapted to high altitudes and extreme cold. It lives on plateaus 16,000 feet (5,000 m) high or more. The species, in the process of becoming extinct in the wild, is not protected, but no measures can be applied in those regions where surveillance is impossible because of their inaccessibility.

Z

ZOROASTRIANISM: an ancient Persian religion. Its followers worship a supreme god who requires men's good deeds for help in his cosmic struggle against the evil spirit Ahriman.

Chronology

B.C.E.

3000

Start of a pictorial script from which cuneiform was taken

Start of the Bronze Age in the Cyclades

2000

The Aryans reach India

Traditional date of the fall of Troy (1184)

1000

End of the Persian Empire after Alexander the Great's victory at the battle of Gaugameles (331)

Conquest of Egypt by Alexander the Great and founding of the city of Alexandria (332)

0

Earliest references to Buddhists (220)

Construction of Hadrian's Wall to protect the north of the province of Britannia (122)

500

Reign of Songzen Gampo, who makes Lhasa the capital of Tibet (circa 605–649)

Vikings find a settlement in Iceland (870)

1000

Tibet falls under Mongol domination (circa 1200)
Marco Polo begins journey to China (1271)

Christopher Columbus lands in America (1492)

1500

The Mongol chief Altan Khan gives Sonam Gyatso the title Dalai Lama (1578)

Ponce de León lands in Florida (1513)
Balboa is first European to sight Pacific Ocean (1579)

1600

The fifth Dalai Lama, Lobsang Gyatso, succeeds in unifying Tibet and extends his spiritual power over the territory; builds Potala Palace (1617–1682)

Jamestown Colony is settled (1607)
Pilgrims land in Plymouth (1620)
Peter the Great builds St. Petersburg (1690s)

1700

The Manchus seize Tibet (1720)

England and Scotland united as Great Britain (1707)
City of Baltimore founded (1763)
French and Indian War ends (1763)

1800

Manchu domination weakened (circa 1850)
Great Britain imposes protectorate on Sikkim, a tributary state of Tibet

Thomas Jefferson elected U.S. president (1800)
War of 1812
Civil War (1861–1865)

1900
C.E.

Simla Conference (1913–1914): Signature of compromise between Tibet and Britain, with China refusing accord
Chinese troops invade Tibet (1950)
Dalai Lama flees into exile in India (1959)
Tibet officially proclaimed Communist (1965)
Cultural Revolution completes destruction of Tibet's religious culture (1966–1976)
Dalai Lama wins Nobel Peace Prize (1989)

World War I (1914–1918)
World War II (1941–1945)
Korean War (1950–1953)
Vietnam War (1960–1975)

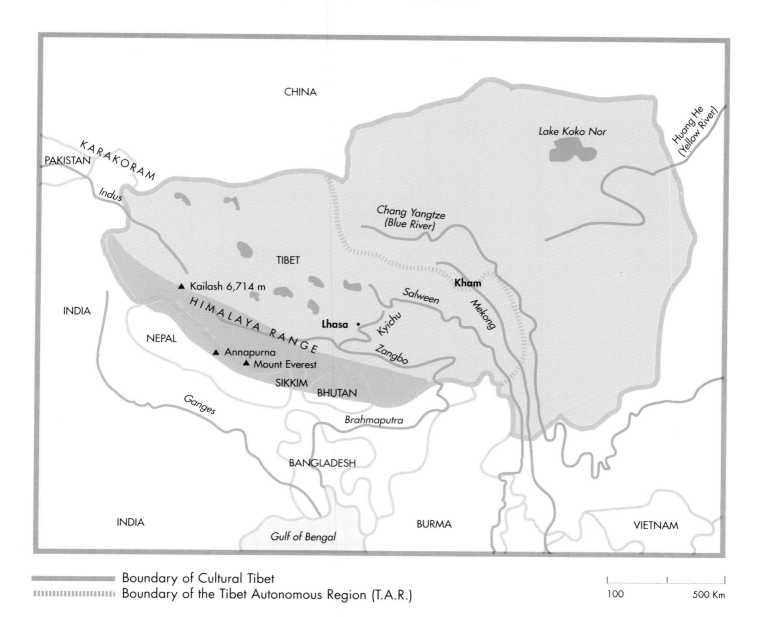

CHINA

KARAKORAM

PAKISTAN

Indus

INDIA

Lake Koko Nor

Huang He
(Yellow River)

Chang Yangtze
(Blue River)

TIBET

▲ Kailash 6,714 m

HIMALAYA RANGE

Kham

Salween

Lhasa •

Kyichu

Mekong

NEPAL

▲ Annapurna
▲ Mount Everest

Zangbo

SIKKIM

BHUTAN

Ganges

Brahmaputra

BANGLADESH

INDIA

BURMA

VIETNAM

Gulf of Bengal

Boundary of Cultural Tibet
Boundary of the Tibet Autonomous Region (T.A.R.)

100   500 Km

TIBET

Area: Tibet Autonomous Region: 471,662 sq. miles (1,221,600 sq. km)
Cultural Tibet: 985,000 sq. miles (1,585,160 sq. km)
Population: estimated at 2 million (T.A.R.)
Capital: Lhasa

Index

Bibliography

TIBET, FOR READERS FROM 7 TO 77

Bell, Charles.
The Religion of Tibet.
Oxford: Oxford University Press, 1931.

Booz, Elizabeth.
Tibet.
Chicago: Passport Books, 1986

The Dalai Lama.
Freedom in Exile.
New York: Harpers, 1992.

The Dalai Lama.
My Land and My People.
New York: Potala Publications, reprinted 1985.

David-Neel, Alexandra.
Initiations and Initiates in Tibet.
Boston: Shambhala Publications, 1970.

Goldstein, Melvyn C.
Nomads of Western Tibet: The Survival of a Way of Life.
Berkeley: University of California Press, 1990.

Gordon, Antoinette K.
Tibetan Religious Art.
New York: Columbia University Press, 1952.

Hume, Lotta Carswell.
Favorite Children's Stories from China and Tibet.
Rutland, Vt.: C. E. Tuttle Co., 1962.

Hyde-Chambers, Fredrick.
Tibetan Folk Tales.
New York: Random House, 1981.

Kalman, Bobbie.
Tibet.
New York: Crabtree Publishing Co., 1990.

Kerr, Blake.
Sky Burial: An Eyewitness Account of China's Brutal Crackdown in Tibet.
Chicago: Noble Press, 1993.

Michael, Franz H.
Rule by Incarnation: Tibetan Buddhism and Its Role in Society and State.
Boulder, Colo.: Westview Press, 1982.

Pilarski, Laura.
Tibet: Heart of Asia.
Indianapolis: Bobbs-Merrill, 1974.

Rhie, Marilyn, and Robert A. F. Thurman
Wisdom and Compassion: The Sacred Art of Tibet.
New York: Abrams, 1991.

Snellgrove, David L.
A Cultural History of Tibet.
New York: F. A. Praeger, 1968.

Sogyal, Rinpoche.
The Tibetan Book of Living and Dying.
San Francisco: Harper San Francisco, 1992.

Thurman, Robert A. F.
The Tibetan Book of the Dead.
New York: Bantam, 1994.

Tucci, Giuseppe.
The Theory and Practice of the Mandala.
New York: Sam Weiser, Inc., 1970

Wilby, Sorrel.
Journey Across Tibet.
Chicago: Contemporary Books, 1988.

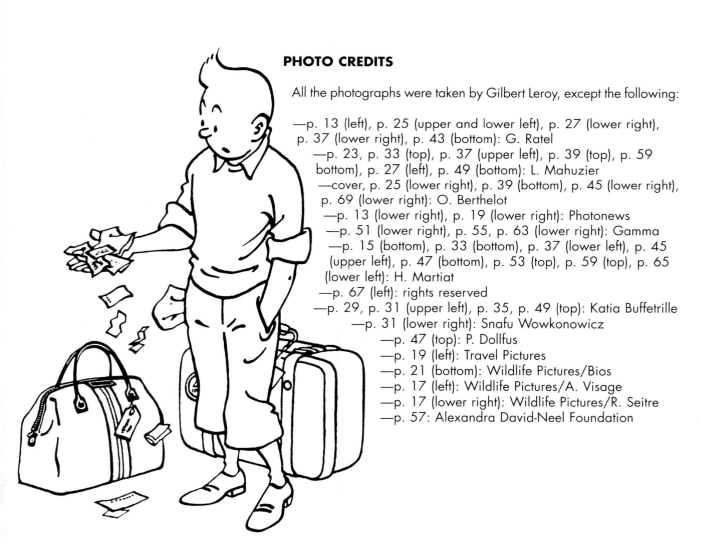

PHOTO CREDITS

All the photographs were taken by Gilbert Leroy, except the following:

—p. 13 (left), p. 25 (upper and lower left), p. 27 (lower right), p. 37 (lower right), p. 43 (bottom): G. Ratel

—p. 23, p. 33 (top), p. 37 (upper left), p. 39 (top), p. 59 bottom), p. 27 (left), p. 49 (bottom): L. Mahuzier

—cover, p. 25 (lower right), p. 39 (bottom), p. 45 (lower right), p. 69 (lower right): O. Berthelot

—p. 13 (lower right), p. 19 (lower right): Photonews

—p. 51 (lower right), p. 55, p. 63 (lower right): Gamma

—p. 15 (bottom), p. 33 (bottom), p. 37 (lower left), p. 45 (upper left), p. 47 (bottom), p. 53 (top), p. 59 (top), p. 65 (lower left): H. Martiat

—p. 29, p. 31 (upper left), p. 35, p. 49 (top): Katia Buffetrille

—p. 31 (lower right): Snafu Wowkonowicz

—p. 47 (top): P. Dollfus

—p. 19 (left): Travel Pictures

—p. 21 (bottom): Wildlife Pictures/Bios

—p. 17 (left): Wildlife Pictures/A. Visage

—p. 17 (lower right): Wildlife Pictures/R. Seitre

—p. 57: Alexandra David-Neel Foundation